SCIENCE STARTERS

Gravity

by Rebecca Pettiford

BLASTOFF!
3
READERS

BELLWETHER MEDIA • MINNEAPOLIS, MN

Note to Librarians, Teachers, and Parents:

Blastoff! Readers are carefully developed by literacy experts and combine standards-based content with developmentally appropriate text.

Level 1 provides the most support through repetition of high-frequency words, light text, predictable sentence patterns, and strong visual support.

Level 2 offers early readers a bit more challenge through varied simple sentences, increased text load, and less repetition of high-frequency words.

Level 3 advances early-fluent readers toward fluency through increased text and concept load, less reliance on visuals, longer sentences, and more literary language.

Level 4 builds reading stamina by providing more text per page, increased use of punctuation, greater variation in sentence patterns, and increasingly challenging vocabulary.

Level 5 encourages children to move from "learning to read" to "reading to learn" by providing even more text, varied writing styles, and less familiar topics.

Whichever book is right for your reader, Blastoff! Readers are the perfect books to build confidence and encourage a love of reading that will last a lifetime!

This edition first published in 2019 by Bellwether Media, Inc.

No part of this publication may be reproduced in whole or in part without written permission of the publisher. For information regarding permission, write to Bellwether Media, Inc., Attention: Permissions Department, 6012 Blue Circle Drive, Minnetonka, MN 55343.

Library of Congress Cataloging-in-Publication Data

Names: Pettiford, Rebecca, author.
Title: Gravity / by Rebecca Pettiford.
Description: Minneapolis, MN : Bellwether Media, Inc., 2019. | Series: Blastoff! Readers. Science Starters
    | Includes bibliographical references and index. | Audience: 5-8. | Audience: K to 3.
Identifiers: LCCN 2017061630 (print) | LCCN 2018009245 (ebook) | ISBN 9781681035406 (ebook)
    | ISBN 9781626178076 (hardcover ; alk. paper) | ISBN 9781618914637 (pbk. ; alk. paper)
Subjects: LCSH: Gravity–Juvenile literature. | Matter–Properties–Juvenile literature.
Classification: LCC QC178 (ebook) | LCC QC178 .P475 2019 (print) | DDC 531/.14–dc23
LC record available at https://lccn.loc.gov/2017061630

Editor: Christina Leaf   Designer: Josh Brink

Printed in the United States of America, North Mankato, MN

Table of
Contents

An Invisible Force

Throw a ball into the air and it falls to Earth. What makes it fall? Gravity.

4

You cannot see gravity, but it is important. It keeps you from flying off the Earth!

What Is Gravity?

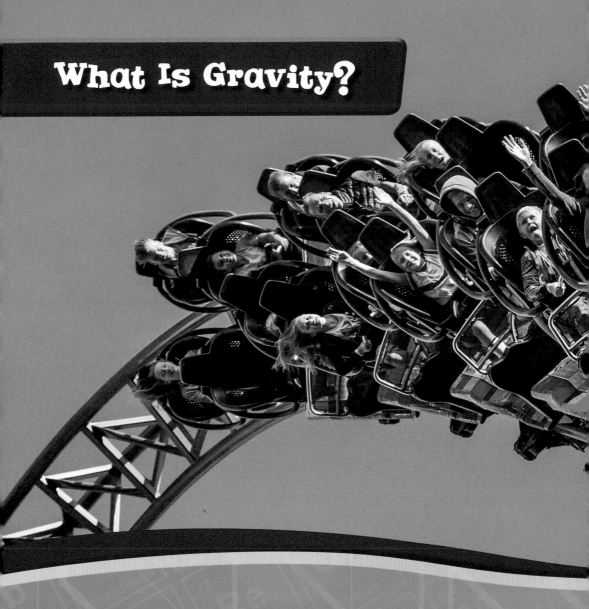

Gravity is a **force** that pulls on everything in the **universe**. It exists between any two objects that have **mass**.

Even people have gravity! It is hard to notice. The gravity we have is overpowered by Earth's gravity.

Gravity is affected by mass. The more mass objects have, the harder gravity pulls.

If a person's mass doubles, gravity will pull on that person twice as hard.

Distance also affects gravity.
As distance increases,
gravity decreases.

The sun has a lot of mass but is far from Earth. Its gravity is not strong enough to pull Earth in completely. Instead, it keeps Earth in **orbit**.

Mass, Distance, and Gravity

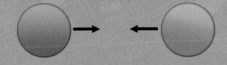

gravity between two objects

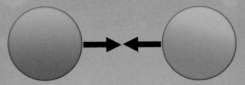

more mass = more gravity

farther distance = less gravity

Gravity and Weight

scale

The force of gravity is measured as weight. With less gravity, objects weigh less even if their mass does not change. This is because gravity pulls with less force.

On a mountaintop,
you weigh a tiny bit
less because there
is less gravity.

The moon has less gravity than Earth. **Astronauts** weigh less there than they do on Earth.

How Does Weight Change?

55 pounds

9.1 pounds

Earth

Moon

People would weigh more on planets with more mass. If we could visit Jupiter, we would weigh more than twice what we weigh here!

Black holes have a lot of mass within a small space. Their **gravitational pull** is extremely powerful.

Nothing can escape the gravitational pull of a black hole. Not even light!

Gravity in Our Lives

Gravity affects more than just weight. The moon's gravitational pull creates **tides**. As the moon circles Earth, tides move water inland and back out.

Tides affect ocean **currents**. Knowing about tides is important for **navigation** and swimming safety.

DANGER

STRONG CURRENT

Penalty as Prescribed

By Order General Manager

Without gravity, buildings, people, and animals would float away. There would be nothing to keep them in place. Gravity is important to all life forms on Earth. It keeps us grounded!

Cup Drop

You can see gravity in action for yourself! Try this activity outside or over a sink.

What you will need:
- a paper cup
- water

1. Poke a hole close to the bottom of the cup. Cover it with your finger.
2. Fill the cup with water.
3. Take your finger away from the hole. The water spills out.

What happened?
Gravity pulls on the cup and the water. Because you are holding the cup, only the water can move freely.

4. Fill the cup again. Cover the hole with your finger.
5. Drop the cup to the ground.

What happened?
The cup and water drop at the same speed. The water is not forced out of the hole.

Glossary

astronauts—people who travel in space

black holes—invisible regions in space that have a strong gravitational pull

currents—the continuous movement of water in the same direction

force—strength or power

gravitational pull—the attraction that an object has on another object

mass—the amount of matter in an object

navigation—the act of finding the way to get to a place when traveling

orbit—the curved path an object takes around another object; Earth orbits the sun.

tides—the regular rise and fall of ocean levels caused by the gravitational pull of the sun and the moon on Earth

universe—everything in space including stars, planets, and galaxies